FIELDS AND HEDGEROWS

Michael Chinery

KINGFISHER BOOKS

A Grassland Walk

Dropping down from the brow of the hill, the footpath passes through rough grassland. A couple of rabbits scuttle away as you approach, and a grass snake slithers noiselessly out of sight. It will be back to continue sunbathing on the path when you have gone. The well-worn track is as hard as rock, but daisies and greater plantains manage to survive there. Their leaves lie flat on the ground and come to little harm if you tread on them, but the flowers are short and stunted. A song thrush has chosen a flat stone on the path as an anvil on which to break snail shells. Look at the broken shells around the stone. If you keep quiet the thrush may return to hammer another one open: she may even bring her young so that they can learn how to break the shells and get at the soft snails inside.

The surrounding grassland, grazed by only a few rabbits, has grown quite tall. It is dotted with wild flowers which attract meadow brown and common blue butterflies. Watch how their hair-like tongues probe the flowers to reach the sweet nectar. In the shadow of the hedge the hogweed spreads its flower-heads like a group of lace-covered tables, and many insects come to lap up the nectar. Purple knapweed mingles with the hogweed, but a marbled white butterfly has no trouble in finding its nectar-filled flowers.

As you approach the stile a magnificent scene unfolds. Much of the land is cultivated, but in the distance you can see the rough grazings on the hillsides. Too steep for ploughing, these slopes have been grazed by sheep for centuries and this has prevented any trees from growing. Look at the brilliant red poppies bordering the wheat field close to the

The Country Code

1. Leave no litter.
2. Fasten all gates.
3. Avoid damaging fences, hedges and walls.
4. Guard against all risk of fire.
5. Keep dogs under proper control.
6. Keep to paths across farmland.
7. Safeguard water supplies – do not dump rubbish in ponds and streams.
8. Protect wildlife, wild plants and trees.
9. Go carefully on country roads.
10. Respect the life of the countryside.

3

A Grassland Walk

The Grasshopper's Song

Male grasshoppers, which you can recognize by the upturned tip of the abdomen, 'sing' to attract females. The 'song' is produced by rubbing the back legs against the wings. Tiny pegs on the inside of the legs make the sound as they pass over a hard vein on each wing. You can make similar sounds by drawing the teeth of a comb over your thumb nail. Each kind of grasshopper has its own 'song'.

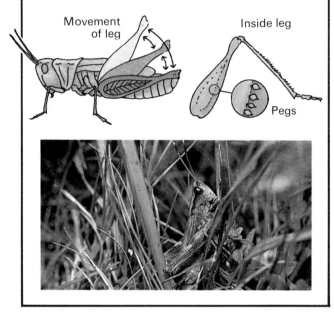

Movement of leg

Inside leg

Pegs

stile. The farmer sprays his crops to kill these weeds, but those on the margin often escape. More will come up the next year, and the next, for poppies scatter huge numbers of seeds which can survive in the soil for a long time, perhaps for as long as a hundred years. Every year the plough turns up another batch ready to grow.

Lower down, on the rich soils of the valley, you can see the haymaking in full swing in the meadows and the cattle grazing peacefully on the pastures. Few flowers grow in these fields because the farmer sows special grass seed mixtures to provide rich food for his cattle. Notice the hedges dividing the fields. Some are very old, for the land has been cultivated for many centuries. We need to grow food in the fields, but the wise farmer makes sure that hedges and other areas remain for wild plants and animals.

To explore and understand the wildlife of all the grassland habitats seen on this walk you will need very little equipment apart from your eyes and a notebook for recording observations and experiments. A hand lens ($\times 10$ is a practical size) will be very useful for close examinations as well as binoculars (see page 19) for watching and identifying birds and other animals from a distance.

Growing Uninvited Guests

Lots of hooked fruits cling to your socks and other clothes during a country walk. Some common ones are shown here Try growing some in a seed tray. The hooks are really designed to cling to animal fur, and by the time they fall off they are a long way from their original homes. This is how the plants spread to new areas. You can also carry seeds in the mud on your shoes. Scrape the mud into a seed tray and see how many plants grow from it.

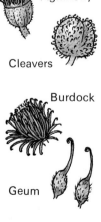

Common Agrimony

Cleavers

Burdock

Geum

Grasses of the Field

Dozens of different kinds of grasses grow in the fields and on the open hillsides and roadside verges. They all look much alike until their flower-heads shoot up in June, and then you can usually pick out several different kinds even in a small area. Some of the commoner grasses are illustrated below. Notice how the flower-heads differ. Some form narrow spikes, others form clusters or graceful sprays. Each flower-head consists of a number of oval spikelets, and each spikelet is composed of papery scales enclosing one or more tiny flowers. The scales are green at first, but become brown or golden as the seeds ripen. The flowers have no petals and no scent or nectar. They rely on the wind to carry pollen from flower to flower for pollination. Until this happens no seeds can develop.

Most grass flowers have three stamens and two feathery stigmas. Look closely at the grasses when their flowers open and you will see the stamens hanging from the spikelets and swaying in the slightest breeze. Pollen is blown from them and some lands on the stigmas to trigger off the development of the seeds. Unfortunately for many people, breathing the grass pollen up their noses causes the unpleasant condition known as hay fever. The months of June and July are the worst for this, because this is when most of the grasses are in flower.

The whole flower-head and stalk dies when the seeds have been scattered, and in the annual grasses the whole plant dies, leaving just the seeds for the following year. Our cultivated cereals, which are simply grasses with large edible grains, are of this type. But most grasses are perennials and, although the old flower-heads die, plenty of leafy shoots remain at the base. Some of these will produce the next year's flower-heads.

Some grasses form thick tufts, while others produce a continuous turf. Grazing, as long as

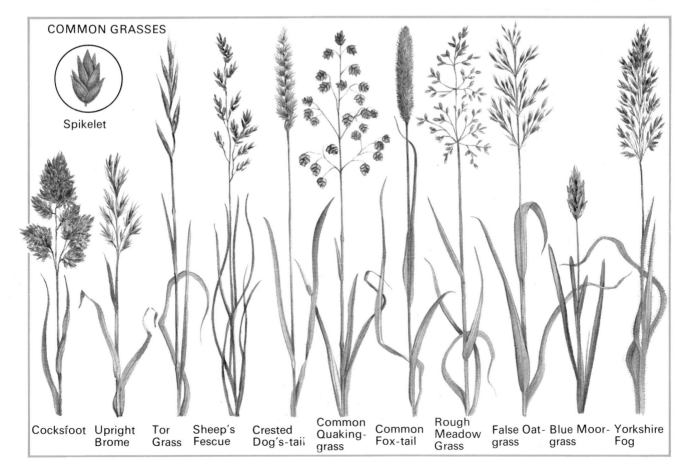

COMMON GRASSES

Spikelet

Cocksfoot | Upright Brome | Tor Grass | Sheep's Fescue | Crested Dog's-tail | Common Quaking-grass | Common Fox-tail | Rough Meadow Grass | False Oat-grass | Blue Moor-grass | Yorkshire Fog

Field Projects

Fields and Meadows

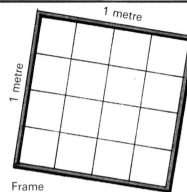

The grassland community differs from place to place. Some plants like dry ground and some prefer damp areas, some like sandy soils and others like chalk. You can explore the differences between various fields by counting the numbers of each plant species in a square metre. Make a simple frame, 1-metre square, as shown in the picture. The strings, 25 centimetres apart, help with the counting, but are not essential. Throw the frame down at random several times in each field and list the plants you find in each square. A field guide will help you to identify them even when they are not in flower. Fields with more flowers than others are likely to be grazed less often.

Pressing Wild Flowers

Picking and pressing wild flowers for a collection is a good way of learning about the many different kinds of flowers. Learn to recognize them from the shapes of the petals and leaves and from the numbers of petals and stamens.

The easiest way to preserve the flowers is to press them under a pile of books. Arrange the flowers neatly between sheets of clean blotting paper, cover them with some sheets of newspaper, and then add some heavy books. Change the paper after a few days if it is damp. The plants should be dry after a couple of weeks and you can then transfer them to a loose-leaf notebook. Label each one carefully. Pick only the common flowers that you see around you.

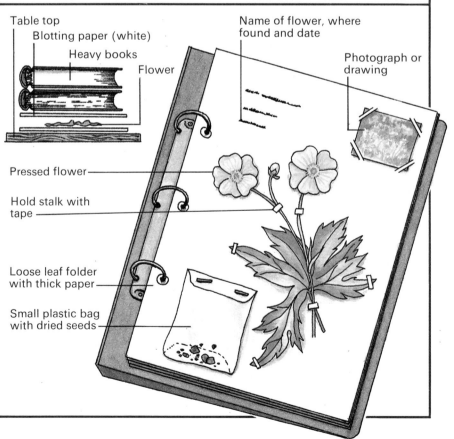

it is not too severe, helps to form turf because it encourages new shoots to spread out at ground level. Mowing does the same. Notice how quickly the grass grows again after grazing or mowing. The leaves grow continuously from the base and soon make good the damage. If they could not do this, grasses could not survive regular grazing.

Grassland Flowers

The majority of our grasslands have been created by sheep grazing during the last few thousand years and are not truly natural. They nevertheless support huge numbers of wild flowers, especially on the unploughed hillsides and commons. You will be surprised at the number of different kinds of flowers that you can find if you really look. Use a good guide book to help you to name them. Explore as many different kinds of grassland as you can and see which kinds of flowers grow in each place.

Examine footpaths and other heavily trampled areas of grassland. You will find fewer kinds of plants here than in the untrodden areas because not many can withstand the constant passage of feet. Among those that can survive on the paths are the dandelion, the greater plantain and the little daisy. Their leaf rosettes lie flat on the ground and are not damaged when you tread on them. If you have plantains on your lawn, try digging a couple up and replanting them in a shady corner of the garden. You will find that they produce much larger, upright leaves, showing that it is the exposure to full light that keeps them flat in trampled areas.

The greatest variety of wild flowers is to be found in lightly grazed areas and also in some ancient hay meadows. Where there is no grazing at all the taller grasses quickly swamp the shorter flowers and, as we shall see later, bushes and trees soon invade the grassland. Heavy grazing, just like regular trampling,

Protected Flowers

Never dig up wild flowers for your garden or for any other reason. This spoils the countryside for other people and is against the law in Britain. Many of our wild flowers have become rare because thoughtless people dug them up in the past. Some of our rarest species must not even be picked: they can't set seeds if you pick them. Never pick unusual flowers – only the ones you know are common.

Right: This picture taken from ground level, reveals the wealth of plant life there is in a meadow. Tall grasses tower above the grassland 'jungle', with bird's-foot trefoil and field mouse-ear growing beneath them. Explore the grassland at ground level yourself.

Grassland Flowers

also destroys most of the flowers. If the grazing is particularly severe – around rabbit warrens, for example – even the grass may be destroyed.

In the lightly grazed areas many of the flowers spring from low-growing mats or rosettes of leaves. These ground-hugging leaves get plenty of light because the grasses around them are regularly nibbled and kept quite short, but the mats and rosettes themselves are rarely eaten. Good examples of these low-growing plants include the wild thyme, cowslip and rockrose – all of which are pictured on the right. Low growth is particularly useful on the drier grasslands, for the leaves then escape the worst of the wind and do not lose as much water. Many of the plants growing on the chalk hills, which are well-drained and often very dry in the summer, have extremely long roots. The roots of the salad burnet, for example, may plunge down more than 60 centimetres. They will always find water at such depths.

Shiny yellow buttercups dot the fields and hillsides from early spring until the autumn. Look carefully at the flowers and you will see that there are two common species. The meadow buttercup likes rich and slightly damp soil. It has smooth flower stalks and its sepals cradle the petals when the flowers open. The bulbous buttercup prefers drier grasslands, especially on lime-rich soils. Its flower stalks are grooved and its sepals turn down when the flowers are open. The bulbous buttercup has usually finished flowering by the end of June.

The Curious Orchids

Many orchids grow in the grasslands of Europe. They are not as showy as their tropical cousins, but their flowers are still fascinating. The bee orchid, which you can

Right: These flowers can all be found in fields, meadows and roadside verges. The rockrose, meadow clary and bee orchid grow only on lime-rich soils. The snake's-head fritillary is very rare: never pick it if you are lucky enough to find one. Look for it in old damp meadows.

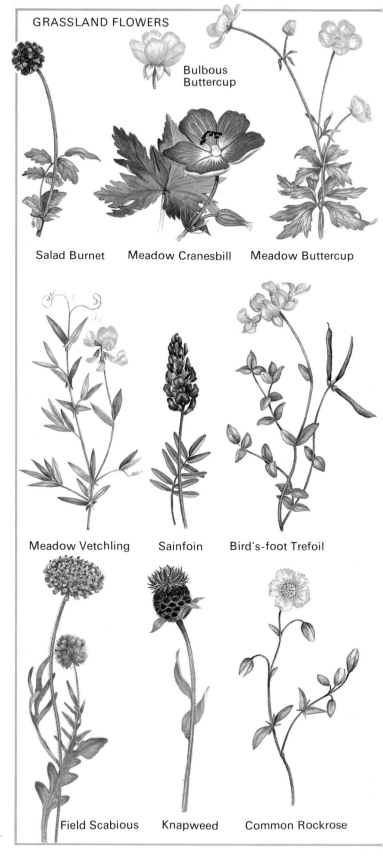

GRASSLAND FLOWERS

Bulbous Buttercup

Salad Burnet   Meadow Cranesbill   Meadow Buttercup

Meadow Vetchling   Sainfoin   Bird's-foot Trefoil

Field Scabious   Knapweed   Common Rockrose

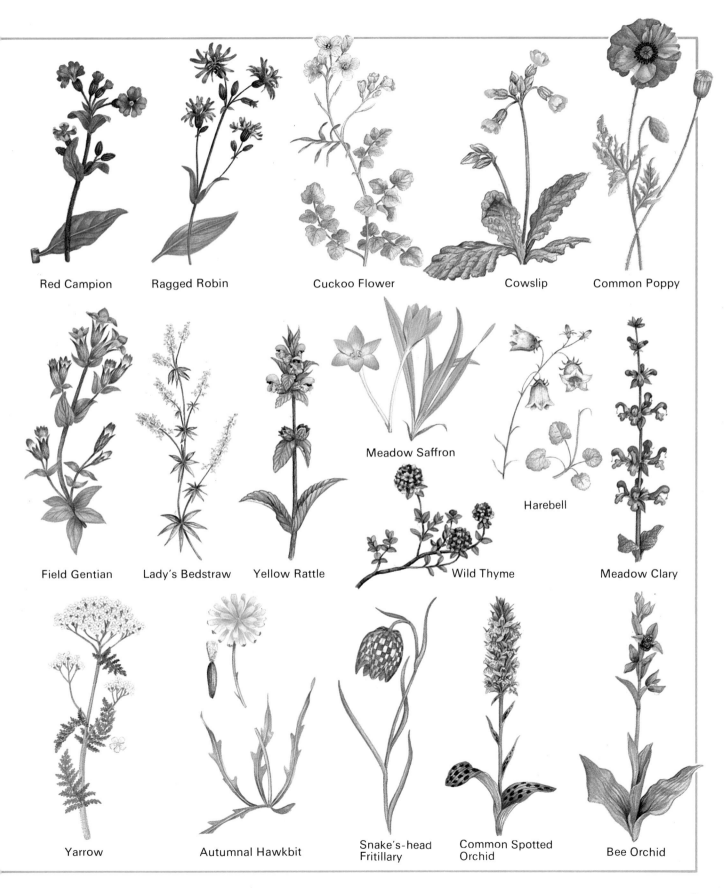

Red Campion

Ragged Robin

Cuckoo Flower

Cowslip

Common Poppy

Field Gentian

Lady's Bedstraw

Yellow Rattle

Meadow Saffron

Harebell

Wild Thyme

Meadow Clary

Yarrow

Autumnal Hawkbit

Snake's-head Fritillary

Common Spotted Orchid

Bee Orchid

see on page 9, has a flower that looks just like a bee. The man orchid has a yellowish flower resembling a tiny man hanging from the stalk, while the lady orchid flower is shaped just like a woman wearing a wide skirt.

Insects of the Grassland

Huge numbers of insects live amongst the grasses and other plants of the fields. Use nets like the ones shown below to catch some of the insects: you will be amazed at how many different kinds occur in just a small area. Get down on your knees and examine the ground around the bottoms of the grasses. Lots of small insects live here, feeding on dead and decaying leaves and other rubbish. Many also rest here during the day and crawl up the plants to feed at night.

If you walk through any rough grassland in the summer you will hear the grasshoppers chirping to each other. Turn back to page 4 to find out how they make their buzzing sounds. Some of them whirr just like miniature sewing machines. The grasshoppers fly up when you walk through the grass, but soon settle again and are very difficult to spot because their green and brown bodies blend so well with the grasses. This camouflage protects the grasshoppers from birds and lizards, which are their main enemies. Some continental grasshoppers have bright red or blue hind wings which show up clearly in flight. When the insects drop to the ground again they cover the hind wings with their drab brown front wings and become very hard to find. Birds which have been following

Using a Sweep Net

Grasshoppers, caterpillars and other insects living in the grass can be collected with a sturdy net called a sweep net. Don't use an ordinary butterfly net for this because it would soon get damaged. Sweep the net from side to side through the vegetation in front of you. Examine it after every two or three sweeps to see what you have caught. You will find lots of spiders and small flies in the net. Use your lens to have a close look at them.

Using a Butterfly Net

A butterfly net can be used to catch all sorts of flying insects. You can buy one or make one. The frame should be at least 30 centimetres across and the bag should be about 60 centimetres deep so that you can fold it over to trap the insects that you catch. Make the bag from fine netting. Black and dark green are the best colours. Be careful not to snag the net on brambles. It is often easier to catch a butterfly on the wing than one sitting on flowers.

Breeding Caterpillars

Caterpillars are easy to rear if you have plenty of the right food plant. An old sweet jar makes a good container: cover the mouth with fine netting. The food plant can be fixed into moist Oasis, or you can put it in a small jar of water. Plug the neck with tissue to stop the caterpillars from getting into the water. Put fresh food plant in each day.

The butterfly pictured here is a small tortoiseshell, whose caterpillars are found on stinging nettles in July. If you keep them

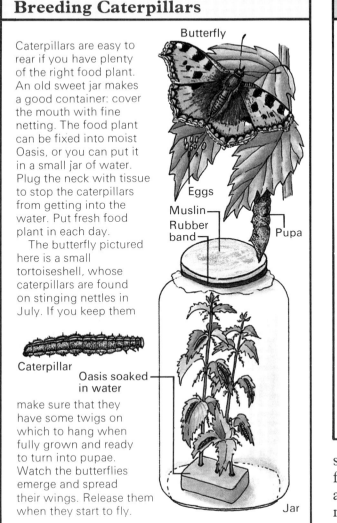

Butterfly

Eggs

Muslin

Rubber band

Pupa

Caterpillar

Oasis soaked in water

Jar

make sure that they have some twigs on which to hang when fully grown and ready to turn into pupae. Watch the butterflies emerge and spread their wings. Release them when they start to fly.

The Meadow Brown Butterfly

The meadow brown is one of our commonest butterflies. You can see it flitting rather lazily over all kinds of grassland in the summer. The one in the picture is feeding at a thistle. Notice its slender tongue probing the flower for nectar. Notice also the eye-spot near the wing-tip. Birds peck at this instead of the real eye: the wing is damaged but the insect is not really hurt.

the bright colours are totally confused. Many people are also puzzled, thinking they have seen brightly coloured butterflies disappear without trace.

Walking through the grasslands in late spring or early summer, watch out for blobs of white froth on the plants. Often there are so many that you get your legs wet. Generally known as cuckoo-spit, the froth has nothing in fact to do with cuckoos. Look inside one of the blobs and you will find a small green insect. It is a young froghopper, which feeds by sucking sap from the plant through its needle-like beak. It surrounds itself with the froth to shield it from the dry air. The froth also gives some protection against birds, but

some enemies know that a juicy insect can be found under the bubbles. Adult froghoppers are small brown jumping insects, not unlike miniature frogs. You will find lots in your sweep net. They suck sap but do not live under froth. You will also find some black and red froghoppers whose bold pattern warns birds that they are not nice to eat. Bold patterns and bright colours like this are known as warning colours.

Grassland Butterflies

Flowery hillsides and roadside verges teem with butterflies in the summer. The insects are attracted by the sweet nectar of knapweeds, thistles, and many other flowers. Some well-known grassland butterflies are illustrated on page 13. The meadow brown (above) is one of the commonest species. It belongs to the family known as the browns. All members of the family have eye-spots around the edges of their wings. The gatekeeper or hedge brown is very common along hedgerows and the edges of woods in southern Britain. Despite its colour, the marbled white also belongs to the brown family: look for its eye-spots. It is especially fond of knapweed and scabious flowers. All the caterpillars in this family feed on grasses.

The swallowtail is extremely rare in Britain, and is only found in a small area of the Norfolk Broads. On the continent, however, many can be seen on dry grassland as well as in damper areas. The scarce swallowtail is actually common on rough grassland in southern Europe.

Several kinds of blue butterfly can be found in grassland. The females are often brown, sometimes with just a few blue scales close to the body. The caterpillars of this group often feed on clovers and vetches. The skippers are fast-flying little butterflies that dart from flower to flower so quickly that you often lose sight of them. They often sit on the flowers with their wings half open.

Moths of Grasslands

Moths are even more common than butterflies, but most of them fly at night and you normally see them only if you disturb them as you walk. The brightly coloured burnet moths fly by day, however, and are often thought to be butterflies. Look for them on the flowers of scabious and knapweed. You can often pick them up, as they are rather sleepy insects. Their bright red spots warn birds that they have a very nasty taste, and the birds soon learn to avoid them. Examine the grass stalks in June for their papery yellow cocoons: you might see the burnet moths emerging from them.

The cinnabar moth is another black and red moth with a nasty taste, although this moth generally flies by night. Watch out for its

Right: The silken tents of the caterpillar of the small ermine moth are common on hedgerows in spring. Notice how the caterpillars have eaten all the leaves in the tent. The adult moth is a delicate insect with black dots all over its white wings. Several other kinds of caterpillars make tent webs.

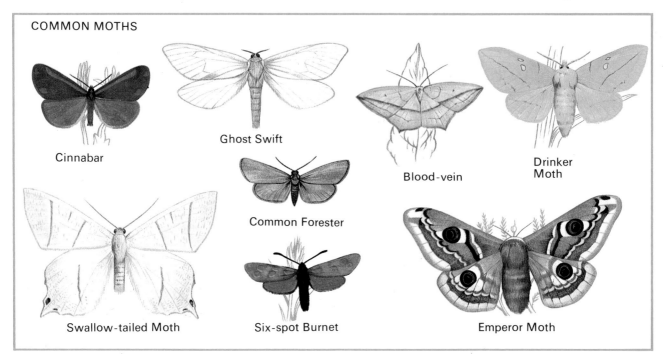

COMMON MOTHS

Cinnabar

Ghost Swift

Common Forester

Swallow-tailed Moth

Six-spot Burnet

Blood-vein

Drinker Moth

Emperor Moth

COMMON BUTTERFLIES

Dark Green Fritillary

female

Gatekeeper

male

male

caterpillar

Marbled White

caterpillar

female

male

male

male

Dingy Skipper

male

Clouded Yellow

Orange Tip

female

Common Blue

female

Small Heath

caterpillar

female

Small Copper

caterpillar

Swallowtail

male

Large Skipper

male

Chalk Blue Hill

Great Banded Grayling

Scarce Swallowtail

Grizzled Skipper

Beetles and Snails

black and gold caterpillars on ragwort plants in July. The caterpillars also taste bad and birds avoid them.

Male emperor moths fly in the sunshine, generally in the afternoon, and can be seen skimming very fast over scrubby grassland and along hedgerows in April and May. They are using their huge feathery antennae to sniff out the plumper and greyer females. The latter do not fly until nightfall, when they lay their eggs on various kinds of plants.

The ghost moth flies at dusk in the summer and gets its name because of the male's eerie flight. The male is pure white on the upper side and dark brown below. As it dances up and down, you see only flashes of white. The yellowish female is attracted to the 'dance' and the insects then mate.

Beetles of all Sizes

Your sweep net will capture large numbers of beetles as you work your way through the grasses and other plants. Many of these beetles will be very small but you can easily recognize them by their hard wing cases covering most of the body. These wing cases are often very shiny, but if you look at them through a hand lens you will see that some are coated with minute scales. Many of the beetles belong to the group known as weevils. You can recognize these by the long snout.

Look for larger beetles crawling on the ground. The bloody-nosed beetle is a rather round black beetle that gives out a drop of bright red blood from its mouth when you squeeze it. This habit is thought to frighten birds that peck at it. If there are rabbits in the area you might well find the shiny black minotaur beetle. This is one of the dung beetles and it buries rabbit droppings as food for both adult and young. The male has a long horn on each side of the thorax (the middle of the three main body sections) and a shorter one in the centre.

Watch for glow-worms on summer evenings just as it is getting dark. The female sits on the grass and gives out a greenish light from her hind end. She may put her light out if you pick her up, but she often goes on glowing. She has no wings and looks rather like a brown woodlouse, but she is actually a beetle. The male has wings and looks much more like a beetle, although his wing covers are quite soft. He flies over the grassland and is attracted to the female's light. Young glow-worms feed on snails.

Grassland Refuse Disposal

The brightly coloured beetle in this picture is a burying beetle or sexton beetle, one of nature's huge army of scavengers which get rid of dung and the bodies of dead animals. Burying beetles work in pairs in the breeding season and quickly bury the bodies of small animals like the shrew seen here. They do this by digging the soil from below the corpses. They then feed on the flesh, and also lay their eggs on or near the flesh so that their grubs have plenty to eat.

In some southern parts of Europe you might be lucky enough to see the glow-worm's cousin the firefly. Both the male and the female have wings, although the female does not fly, and both produce light. The males fly low over the ground and produce short flashes of light every second. The females sit in the grass and reply with their own flashes. The males then come down and the beetles mate.

Grassland Snails

Snails need plenty of lime to make their shells and are most common in chalky areas and on other lime-rich soils. Most of them feed on dead and rotting leaves. The brown-lipped snail is one of the commonest. Its shell is usually yellow or pink, with up to five brown bands on each whorl. The lip is brown. The white-lipped snail is very similar except for its white lip. Both are commonly called banded snails. The shell of the striped snail is also rather similar, although its shell is basically white. If you turn it upside down you will see a narrow hole called the umbilicus. In the banded snails this hole is completely covered by the lip. The striped snail often clusters on plants in dry weather.

Keep a special watch for the round-mouthed snail on chalk and limestone. It is one of the few land snails that close their shells with a horny disc like that of the winkle.

Snakes and Lizards

The snakes and lizards belong to the large group of animals called reptiles. They are generally described as cold-blooded animals, but their bodies actually stay at the same

A Thrush's Anvil

Thrush

Broken shells

Anvil

Look for the song thrush's anvil – a large stone, often at the side of a path, on which the bird hammers open snail shells. Examine the broken shells. Most of them belong to the banded snails and are yellowish with up to five brown bands. Some have no bands at all. Work out which shells are the best camouflaged on rough grassland. Which shells are most often collected by the thrush? Try to find living snails in the grass yourself.

Above: Examine grassland snail shells for glow-worm grubs. Here is one eating into a snail.

Below: If you find a snake watch how it picks up scent by flicking its tongue out. This is a grass snake.

Snakes and Lizards

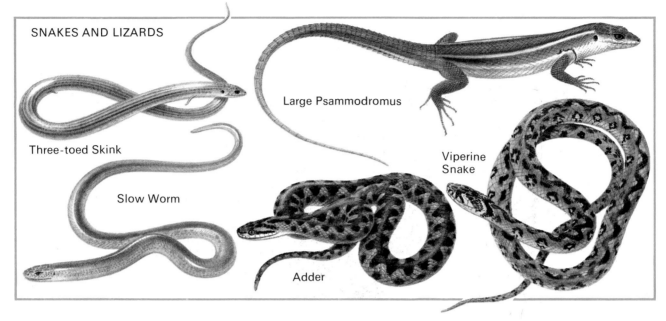

SNAKES AND LIZARDS

Three-toed Skink

Slow Worm

Large Psammodromus

Viperine Snake

Adder

temperature as the surroundings and are sometimes quite hot. They are very sluggish in cold weather, and they sleep right through the winter in Europe. Only three kinds of snakes and three kinds of lizards live in Britain, but there are many more in the warmer parts of Europe. Most like to

Sun-loving Lizards

This wall lizard is living up to its name and enjoying a spot of sunbathing on an old wall. If you approach very carefully, with no sudden movement, you can get quite close to basking lizards. Be careful not to let your shadow fall on them or they will dart away in a flash and may not reappear for a long time.

sunbathe in the mornings to warm up, and this is a good time to look for them. As they get warm, they get much more active and more difficult to find – you may see only a tail disappearing into the grass. All the reptiles have scaly skins and they are not at all slimy.

Snakes have no legs, but they glide very efficiently over the ground. They like to coil around clumps of grass or the base of bushes for sunbathing. Walk quietly if you want to see them, for they can pick up the vibrations of your footsteps and may be frightened away. The adder is the only poisonous snake in Britain. You can recognize it by the dark zig-zag pattern on its back. It lives on both dry and damp grassland and feeds on lizards and small mammals. The grass snake prefers damp grassland and is common around ponds and streams. It swims well and frogs are its favourite prey. Look for the yellowish collar to identify this snake.

Lizards are generally very agile and difficult to catch, but make good pets if you have a suitable cage such as an old fish tank. They like rough grassland with rocky areas or bare ground for sunbathing. Many live on and around walls in the southern parts of Europe and are known as wall lizards. Watch them dart after insects, which are the main foods of most lizards. The viviparous lizard is the commonest British species. Its eggs hatch more or less as they are being laid. Look for the pregnant females basking in the sun to speed up the development of their eggs. The slow-worm is a legless lizard with a liking for lush grassland. It feeds mainly on slugs. Look for it after rain, or else search under flat stones and old planks or sheets of corrugated iron. Don't mistake it for the three-toed skink of southern Europe which looks like a slow worm but has tiny legs.

In southern Europe, keep an eye open for large green lizards. As well as eating insects they sometimes take baby birds and mammals and even gobble up other lizards. Do not be surprised to find lizards without tails. If a lizard is caught by the tail, it can snap it off and escape – leaving the bird or other enemy holding just the wriggling tail. The lizard grows a new tail later.

Birds of the Fields

Walk over farmland or grassy hillsides at any time of the year and you will almost certainly catch a glimpse of the skylark. This is truly a bird of the open spaces, keeping well away from trees and hedgerows and spending all of its time either on the ground or in the air. It feeds on seeds and insects and you can watch it quite easily as it roams over farmland in winter. Your binoculars will pick out the small crest on the head and the white edges to the tail. In spring and summer you are more likely to see the skylark high in the air, although you will probably hear it long before you see it. The males rise almost vertically to heights up to 300 metres and hover there for long periods while pouring out their shrill, warbling song. They usually sing directly above their nests, which are always built on the ground. Do not try to find the nests: they are very well camouflaged and you could easily tread on them without seeing them.

The meadow pipit is another rather drab brown, ground-nesting bird and you might easily mistake it for the skylark. It has no crest, however, and its beak is thinner than that of the skylark. Like the skylark, its drab

Below: The graceful hen harrier swoops over the wilder grasslands. This is a female: the male is grey.

Birds of the Fields

colour camouflages it against predators. The meadow pipit produces its high-pitched trilling song while rising to a height of about 30 metres and then gliding down again. It does not hover. Meadow pipits like most kinds of open country but, unlike the skylark, they do not nest on cultivated land.

The pictures below show some of the many small birds that breed and feed in the grasslands. Several of them nest on the ground but, apart from the skylark, meadow pipit and wheatear, they like to stay close to hedgerows or scattered shrubs. Listen for the song of the yellowhammer, consisting of a series of very short notes followed by a long one. The song is commonly translated as '*a little bit of bread and no chee-ee-ee-se*'.

The birds shown opposite are all larger species than the ones below. Rooks and carrion crows both nest in trees but com-

GRASSLAND BIRDS

Yellowhammer

Linnet

Wheatear

Meadow Pipit

Long-tailed tit

Whitethroat

Redwing

Fieldfare

Stonechat

Skylark

monly feed on farmland. They take some seed from ploughed land, but also devour many harmful insects, such as cockchafer grubs, and snap up insects on cow-pats. Dead animals are also eaten – you often see the birds pecking at rabbits that have been killed on the road. To learn how to spot the difference between a rook and a crow look at their beaks and legs. The hooded crow is really just a form of the carrion crow.

Binoculars for Bird-watching

There are many sizes and models of binoculars on the market. Don't be tempted to go for the biggest and most powerful: these will be very heavy to carry. A pair marked 8×40 giving you a magnification of 8, is ideal for normal bird-watching. If you can afford a lightweight pair, choose one marked 10×24 or thereabouts.

light-breasted form

dark-breasted form

Barn Owl

female

male

Kestrel

Curlew

Carrion Crow

Rook

Hooded Crow

Short-eared Owl

Lapwing

male

female

Partridge

male

female

Pheasant

Birds of Prey

Lapwings, also known as peewits from the sound of their calls, are common on farmland after harvest. Watch them moving across the fields in large flocks as they search for seeds and insects. They often take flight together and perform spectacular aerial displays. You can see the birds on pastures and rough grasslands throughout the year. They nest on the ground where the grasses are not too tall.

Birds of Prey

The open grasslands are superb hunting grounds for many birds of prey. The best known of these hunters is the kestrel, also called the windhover because of the wonderful way in which it hovers almost motionless on the air. Look for it over roadside and motorway verges as well as fields and hillsides, and notice how the tail feathers fan out to give the bird extra lift. Although it might hover as much as 30 metres above the ground, its sharp eyes spot any movement on the ground. Watch how the kestrel plunges down to investigate: you might even see it rise again with a vole securely gripped in its talons. Field voles (see page 22) are the kestrel's main prey and a fully grown bird will usually eat the equivalent of two voles each day. Other foods include mice and shrews, beetles, grasshoppers and small birds.

The hen harrier is a spectacular bird of prey which usually operates over wilder grasslands. Swooping low over the grass, and banking and turning majestically at the end of each run, the bird gradually covers a wide area in its search for food. Small birds and mammals, including rabbits, are the harrier's main prey. Long wings enable the harrier to make quick, elegant turns when it spots one of these and its long legs are lowered to snatch the animal from the ground.

The short-eared owl hunts in much the same way as the harrier and, unlike most other owls, it flies in the daytime. By night, its place is taken by the barn owl, whose white underside gives it a very ghostly appearance as it glides swiftly over the fields. The barn owl can screech and hiss loudly but it is silent when hunting and this makes its flight even more ghostlike.

Observing Rabbits

Rabbits are best seen in the evening or early in the morning, but it is very easy to find out where they live. Look for their burrows, surrounded by lots of bare soil where the animals have chewed away all the turf. As in the photograph above there may be plenty of ragwort instead, which the rabbits don't like and won't eat. Look for other tell-tale signs, such as piles of droppings – often placed on ant hills – and gnawed bark around the bases of trees. The rabbit's two front teeth are grooved in the front edge and when the animals chew bark they leave a narrow strip in the centre of each tooth mark. These animals eat bark mainly during the winter months.

Grassland Mammals

As we have already seen, the grasses are the only plants able to stand up to regular grazing. In areas of natural grassland we find large herds of grazing mammals – bison on the American prairies, antelopes on the African savannas and kangaroos on the Australian grasslands. Apart from some mountain pastures, European grasslands are not natural and so we have no such grazing herds. The largest of our truly wild grazers, other than goats and other mountain animals, are the hares and rabbits.

Look for the brown hare in pastures and rough grassland and also on cultivated land. It is quite easy to spot in grain fields in the spring, before the cereals grow too high. You might even see the hare's famous spring 'boxing matches', in which two or more males chase each other and often stand on their hind legs to fight. This behaviour gave rise to the expression 'mad as a March hare'. Dawn and dusk are the best times for watching hares, but they are often active in the middle of the day in areas where they are not disturbed. The brown hare's ears are much larger than those of a rabbit, and when the animal moves you will see that its legs are also much longer. Whereas the rabbit scuttles along on its short legs, the hare goes in leaps and bounds.

Hares do not make burrows. They sleep on the surface on a flattened area of grass called a form. With their ears pulled down along the back, it is surprising how easily they can hide amongst the grasses. The young, called leverets, are born in a form and, unlike baby rabbits, they are fully furred and have their eyes open.

Mischievous Rabbits

The rabbit was once confined to Spain and Portugal, but has now spread to nearly all parts of Europe. The Normans brought it to Britain in the 12th century. Rabbits can destroy many field crops and young tree plantations and are a serious pest in many areas. The hare can also be a pest, but is generally a solitary animal and does less harm than the rabbits which live in colonies. Each colony inhabits a collection of burrows known as a warren. This is always close to some kind of shelter, in the form of rocks or hedgerows, and never right out in the open. Many rabbits live in the woodland if there are surrounding fields for them to feed in. They are mainly nocturnal but, like the hare, they come out by day in undisturbed areas. Constant nibbling keeps the grass very short around the warren. The ground may be quite bare close to the entrances, but ragwort and stinging nettles may grow here because the rabbits will not eat these plants.

You must keep very still and very quiet if you want to watch rabbits. It is best to use binoculars from a distance. If any rabbits see you they will warn the others by thumping the ground with their hind legs. The bobbing white tails of the scurrying rabbits also warn others of danger. Look for skulls and other bones around the warren. Notice that there

Signs of the Brown Hare

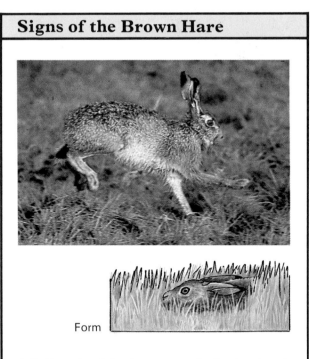

Form

A flattened patch of grass may indicate a hare's form – an area where it rests and even gives birth to its babies called leverets. When resting in its form, the hare lays its long ears back along its body and it is then very hard to see even in fairly short grass. It keeps very still if it senses danger.

Small Mammals

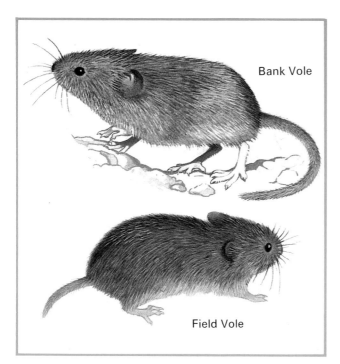

Bank Vole

Field Vole

The Hidden World of the Mole

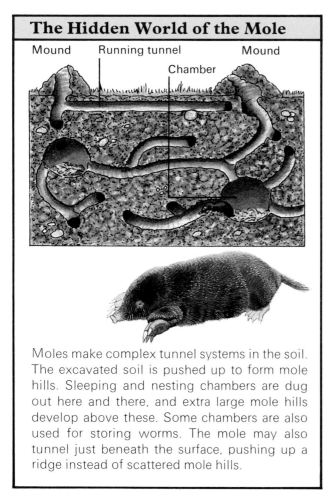

Mound   Running tunnel   Mound

Chamber

Moles make complex tunnel systems in the soil. The excavated soil is pushed up to form mole hills. Sleeping and nesting chambers are dug out here and there, and extra large mole hills develop above these. Some chambers are also used for storing worms. The mole may also tunnel just beneath the surface, pushing up a ridge instead of scattered mole hills.

are two very tiny teeth just behind the big front teeth in the upper jaw. Only rabbits and hares have these extra teeth.

Although rabbits do a lot of damage to crops and young trees, they do help to keep our grasslands open. When most of the rabbits died in the 1950s from a disease called myxomatosis, the open hillsides were quickly taken over by bushes and shrubs: some have now been converted to woodland.

Voles and Moles

The field vole is the commonest grassland mammal in Britain although it cannot survive in heavily grazed areas. Look for its runways criss-crossing the ground under long grass. It also makes narrow tunnels just under the soil surface. This vole feeds mainly on grass, but it is a nuisance in young plantations because it nibbles the soft bark of the sapling trees. Active mostly at night but also by day, it is caught in large numbers by owls and other birds of prey.

The bank vole, distinguished by its brighter, browner coat and longer tail, prefers shrubby areas and hedgerows and never ventures far into the open grassland. Unlike the field vole, it often climbs bushes to eat fruits and insects. Rose hips are among the bank vole's favourite fruits, but it eats only the outer flesh: a naked cluster of pips shows that a bank vole has been at work.

You will not see moles very often because they spend almost all their time eating earthworms under the ground. They always let us know that they are there, however, by pushing up piles of soil here and there – the familiar mole hills. This soil comes from the mole's extensive tunnel system, which it excavates with its massive, shovel-like front feet. You might be lucky enough to see one of the hills being made. The mole uses its head for this and you might even see it push its head right out. The piles of soil soon collapse, especially in wet weather. Do not confuse them with ant-hills, which are also common in fields and meadows. These ant-hills are permanent mounds and usually covered with grass and other plants.

Invading Scrub

In the absence of grazing by rabbits and other animals the grasslands are rapidly colonized by shrubs. Hawthorn and birch are among the

Above: Grasslands undergo huge changes when grazing stops. Tall grasses swamp the smaller ones and with'n a few years bushes begin to appear – having grown from seeds brought by birds or by the wind. This chalk hillside was open grassland only a few years ago.

first to appear, closely followed by brambles and wild roses. Sallow is quick to invade the damper soils, while privet soon springs up on the dry soils of the chalk. If there is an overgrown grassland near you, make a count of the number of different kinds of shrubs. The shrubs shade out most of the low-growing flowering plants, and the whole area may gradually become woodland if people do not intervene and remove the scrub. Changes like these can take place very quickly, as happened when most of the rabbit population in Britain was killed by the myxomatosis outbreak in the 1950s.

Some of our older hedgerows came into existence by a similar process of succession. They sprang up on the no man's land between neighbouring farms or villages and gradually came to serve as boundaries. Other old hedges are the strips of trees and bushes left behind as boundaries when woodlands were cleared for agriculture. But most of today's hedges are much newer, having been planted during the last 200 years to enclose much of the original common land. These newer hedges generally have fewer kinds of shrubs in them and they tend to be much straighter than rambling ancient hedgerows.

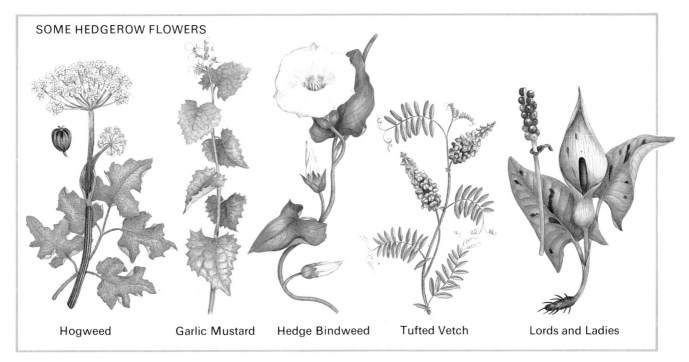

SOME HEDGEROW FLOWERS

| Hogweed | Garlic Mustard | Hedge Bindweed | Tufted Vetch | Lords and Ladies |

A Hedgerow Year

Spring

This flower-rich spring hedgerow is dominated by gorse bushes with their brilliant yellow flowers. The cow parsley is beginning to open and there are buttercup and stitchwort flowers nearer to the ground. Lots of bees are already busy at the flowers. Small oaks and elms are putting out their leaves, while the wild rose is already shooting rapidly into the air. In late spring it will be covered with delicate pink flowers. The dense growth of the hedge is ideal for nesting birds, such as blackbirds, dunnocks and whitethroats. Linnets may also nest in the gorse bushes. Watch carefully for the comings and goings of the birds, but never poke about to find their nests. This hedge is obviously trimmed regularly to keep it low but, if done in winter, this does not affect the birds.

Summer

This ancient hedgerow, seen here in its full summer glory, contains many different kinds of shrubs and herbaceous plants. On the left you can see the wayfaring tree, one of our earliest-fruiting species. You can already see the oval and rather flattened berries beginning to ripen. They are black when fully ripe. Such a hedge will be alive with insects. Search for them by looking for tell-tale signs of chewed leaves: sometimes you will find that whole branches have been stripped by caterpillars. It is just the place to watch for a cuckoo in early summer, swooping to and fro in search of its favourite food – hairy caterpillars. Songthrushes, chaffinches and many other birds will nest in a thick hedge like this. Use your notebook to keep a record of the birds and other animals you find.

Autumn

Autumn is the season for fruit, and in a good year the hedges are weighed down with a colourful assortment of berries and other fruits. This hedgerow is covered with deep red haws, the fruits of the hawthorn. Other common fruits that you might find are the bright orange-red hips of the wild rose, the small black fruits of the dogwood and the wild privet, and of course the delicious blackberries which you can eat and enjoy. But remember that many of the hedgerow fruits are poisonous – even if the birds eat them without harm it does not mean that you can eat them as well. Try to keep a record of which kinds of birds eat which kinds of fruits. Watch the leaves change colour and fall as autumn progresses. You can then see how many birds nested in the hedge and examine the old nests.

Winter

This straight hedgerow, standing leafless in the winter, consists mainly of hawthorn and was obviously planted specifically as a field boundary (see page 23). Most of the haws have been stripped by the birds, but a few remain. As well as our resident thrushes and other fruit-eating birds, fieldfares and redwings from northern Europe arrive to feast on the hedgerow fruits in the winter. Some fruits ripen much earlier than others and are eaten first. Rose hips and the bright red garlands of black bryony berries are some of the latest to disappear. Many people think that a good berry crop indicates a hard winter on the way, but it really shows that the previous year's summer was a good one, for this is when the buds which eventually produced the fruits were formed.

Flowers of the Hedgerow

Hedgerow Flowers

Whatever their origin, the hedgerows contain lots of wild flowers that enjoy shelter. Roadside hedges and verges are good places to see these flowers and some of them tell us the history of the hedge. Bluebells, wood anemones and dog's mercury, for example, indicate that the hedge was certainly once part of a wood.

Cow parsley and hogweed are two very common hedgerow umbellifers – plants that carry umbrella-like heads of small flowers. Cow parsley blooms in late spring and its very delicate white flowers have given it the alternative name of Queen Anne's lace. Hogweed blooms a little later and goes on for much of the summer. Its flowers are larger and its stems are much thicker and rougher than those of the cow parsley. Examine the hogweed's flower-heads for insects. Hundreds of different kinds of flies and beetles gather here to lap up the nectar. You can see the nectar yourself: it forms glistening beads in the centre of the little flowers. Do not muddle the hogweed with the strongly

HEDGEROW CLIMBERS

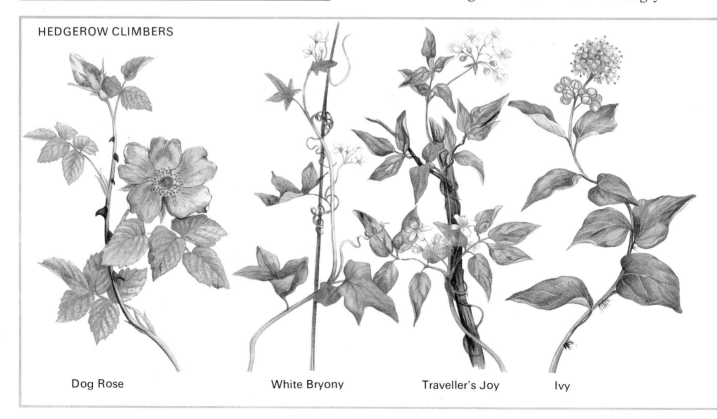

Dog Rose   White Bryony   Traveller's Joy   Ivy

scented yarrow. This also has white flower heads, but the stalks do not all come from the same point as they do in the umbels. Yarrow also has very ferny leaves.

Look for the strange flower spikes of the lords-and-ladies in spring. Their unpleasant smell attracts small flies, which crawl down the spikes and pollinate them. Very poisonous red berries develop later.

Hedgerow Climbers

You will find many climbing plants in the hedgerows and some of the commonest kinds are pictured below. They all have weak stems and need the support of the hedgerow trees and shrubs to grow tall. Try to work out how each kind of climber actually climbs. Examine the tiny hooked prickles on the stems of the goosegrass, or cleavers, that smothers many rural hedgerows – and also clings tightly to your clothes. Black bryony, unrelated to the white bryony shown below, twines around its supports. It is not very obvious in the summer, but when the leaves fall in autumn you can see its brilliant red

berries festooning the bare twigs. You might wonder why these tempting berries are not snapped up by the birds. The truth is that they do not taste pleasant to the birds until well into the winter when their juice has lost its bitter tang. Although birds can eat these berries, they are very poisonous to people and you must leave them alone.

Above: The speckled bush cricket is very common among hedgerow nettles and brambles. The brown 'saddle' of this male is formed from its very short wings.

Honeysuckle   Bramble

Caterpillar Hide-and-Seek

Many hedgerow caterpillars, such as this early thorn caterpillar, are extremely well camouflaged. They look just like twigs and you must look very hard to find them. Even the birds are fooled for much of the time, as long as the caterpillars keep still. They usually feed at night, when the birds are asleep.

Slugs and Snails

The Robin's Pincushion

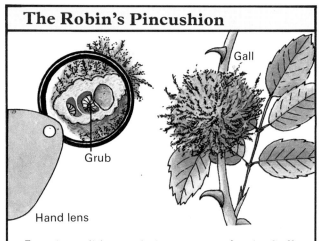

Grub

Hand lens

Gall

Examine wild roses in late summer for the fluffy red or orange growths known as robin's pincushions. These are galls, caused by the presence of tiny insect grubs in the plant's stems or leaves. Cut open a gall with a sharp knife and you will see the grubs, each in its own little chamber. If you collect a gall in early spring and keep it in a jam jar you will be able to see the adult insects come out. They are called gall wasps. Release them on the wild roses and you will get a new crop of pincushions in the summer. Look for other kinds of galls. They occur on many kinds of plants, but oaks are best.

Above: Snails like damp conditions and usually hide away in dry weather, but these striped snails cluster on plant stems in the summer drought. Their shells are sealed with hardened slime to keep in moisture.

Hedgerow Insects

Huge numbers of insects live in the hedge. Many feed on the leaves and flowers, but some are carnivorous and attack the plant-eaters. Search a short stretch of hedgerow carefully and you will be amazed at how many insects you find. Look for tell-tale holes in leaves to show you where caterpillars have been feeding. You will still have to look carefully for the caterpillars because many of them are wonderfully camouflaged. You can keep the caterpillars at home, as described on page 11. Some caterpillars like to bury themselves before turning into pupae, so put a layer of moist peat in the bottom of the cage.

Most of the caterpillars feeding on the shrubs will turn into moths. You can often find the adult moths resting on the hedgerow leaves and twigs by day or you can shake the branches to see what falls out. If you walk along the hedgerow at night you will see some of the moths in flight or feeding at the flowers. By day, of course, it is the butterflies that feed at the flowers. Bramble flowers are particularly attractive to them. Several of the butterflies illustrated on page 13 can be seen in the hedgerow.

Listen for the songs of the bush-crickets – short chirps or prolonged buzzing sounds. These insects are related to the grasshoppers but they have much longer antennae and sing by rubbing their wings together. Unlike grasshoppers, they are often active at night.

Slugs and Snails

Hedgerows, especially those with ditches beside them, make fine homes for slugs and snails. These animals revel in the damp conditions at the bottom of the hedge and grow fat on the decaying leaves. The best way to find them at work is to explore the hedgerow with a torch at night, but you can also find plenty of slugs and snails crawling around after a summer shower in the daytime. Look on roadside verges just after the grass has been cut, for the animals like to feed on the dying grass. Large black slugs are very common here. They may be 15 centimetres long, but if you prod one you will see it shrink

The Spider's Web

Spiders' webs look beautiful when laden with dew or frost in the early morning, but what is really remarkable is the speed and precision with which the webs are built. Search the hedgerow carefully to find a spider at work. Some of the stages are illustrated here. First of all the spider forms a bridge thread across the top (1), then it completes the outer framework (2). The 'spokes' are put in place next (3), and then a central platform (4). The spider finishes off with the sticky spiral threads which actually trap flies and other insects. Some spiders construct new webs each day.

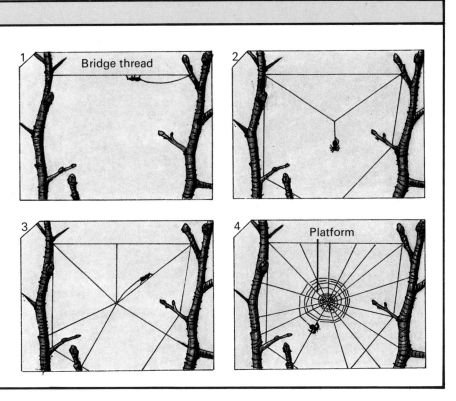

to a black blob and sway from side to side. Notice how sticky your fingers are after touching the slug. The sticky slime helps to keep the slug moist and also protects it from its enemies. You might also see large brown or orange slugs, especially in southern areas. These are just varieties of the large black slug.

The hedgerow snails include many of the banded snails that live on open grassland. Look also for the Kentish snail, whose creamy white shell usually has a reddish brown area near the opening. Watch how the snails glide smoothly over the grass, leaving a trail of slime behind them. The slime helps to lubricate their passage. Put a slug or snail in a jam jar and observe it through the glass. Notice the muscles rippling in the foot as the animal glides along.

Lurking Spiders

The abundant insect life of the hedge provides plenty of food for spiders. Keep a watch on a hedge in the autumn to see just how many spiders live there and wait for insects to land in their webs. The webs show up clearly when laced with dew on autumn mornings. There are many kinds of webs apart from the orb-web seen above. Most numerous are the little hammock webs. These are normally flat or domed, but often sag when laden with dew. Look underneath the web for the little spider. *Linyphia triangularis* is the commonest. It has a row of dark triangles along its back. Look above the hammock to see a network of 'scaffolding'. Small insects bump into these silken threads and fall on to the hammock. The spider then bites them through the web before they can escape. The web is not sticky, but the insects get their feet tangled in it.

Examine the plants by the side of the hedge in the summer for the silken tents of the nursery-web spider. The mother spider fixes her ball of eggs to a plant and then spins the tent over them for protection. She usually sits on the web until the eggs hatch and, as long as you do not make any sudden movements, it is quite easy to watch her. She will scurry away when you get close to see the egg-ball, but she will soon come back. If the eggs have hatched

Hedgerow Mammals

What's in a Nest?

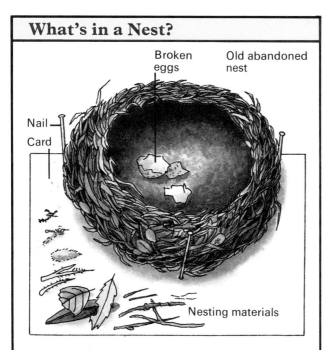

Nail

Card

Broken eggs

Old abandoned nest

Nesting materials

Hedgerow birds build new nests each year and you can safely take down the old nests to examine them in the autumn. Put them into plastic bags with a little moth-proofer for a while to kill the fleas in them. Then you can pull the nests to pieces to see what they are made of. You can even make a collection of old nests if you have room. Put them on stout card or in shoeboxes. Label with the type of nest and where and when you found it. Never take nests unless you are sure they have been abandoned.

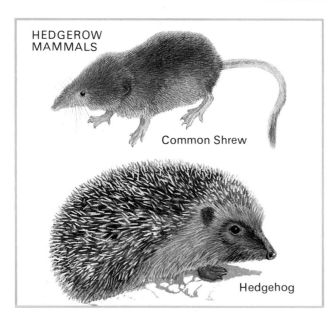

HEDGEROW MAMMALS

Common Shrew

Hedgehog

you might see hundreds of tiny babies in the tent, although they soon scatter to begin their own lives. This kind of spider is a hunter, chasing small insects instead of making a web to trap them.

The Prickly Hedgehog

As dusk falls on the hedgerow the hedgehog wakes up for its nightly ramble. The best way to find it is to listen for its grunting and scuffling as it searches for slugs and other small animals in the leaf litter at the bottom of the hedge. You can then use your torch to pick out this fascinating little mammal. It does not mind the light and may well sit and watch you for a while before ambling off surprisingly quickly. Notice its pointed snout, which helps it to sniff out its food. If the hedgehog is really alarmed it may roll into a prickly ball. This protects it from most of its enemies, but not from motor cars and many hedgehogs can be seen squashed on the roads. It is difficult to discover the hedgehog's footprints in the rough ground of the hedge, but you can sometimes find its long black droppings, usually full of beetle wing cases. Do not forget that hedgehogs go to sleep for the winter: summer and autumn are the best times for looking for them.

The shrews are closely related to the hedgehog. The common shrew is very common in the hedgerow, where it feeds on a wide range of small animals. Listen carefully for its high-pitched squeaks. It is active day and night, but you will not see it very often because it keeps to dense cover.

The Farmer's Fields

All farmland is artificial, but some of the fields are more natural than others. The rough pastures of the uplands are not touched by the plough and the steep slopes are covered with native grasses and other plants which have spread over the hills since the trees disappeared. These rough grazing lands may be divided by stone walls, but are often wide open and the sheep can roam over vast areas.

The lower slopes and most lowland areas are regularly cultivated and their vegetation is far from natural. The pastures where cattle graze may look natural, but most of them have been sown with special mixtures of grass seed to provide the best grasses for the cattle. Native plants gradually invade the fields and the grazing quality gradually falls until the farmer re-seeds the land with the cultivated grasses. Hay meadows are usually treated in the same way. Here the grasses are allowed to grow up and flower in the summer before being cut for hay. Two or even three crops may be taken in some years, especially if the fields are heavily manured or fertilized. Many meadows are now cut for silage. The grass is cut while still green and stored in special pits where it is turned into a sweet 'cake' which the cattle enjoy during the winter.

Clover and lucerne are often sown with the grasses for hay and silage, but you will not find many other flowers in modern hay meadows or leys. There are, however, a number of ancient meadows which have never been ploughed or treated with fertilizer and which still support a wealth of wild flowers. Such meadows are particularly common on hillsides and the best examples can be seen in the Alps.

Food from the Fields

The cereals are the most important of our field crops. They are all large grasses with starch-filled edible grains. Four major cereals are shown on the left below. Watch out for them when you are out and about in the countryside. Look for other kinds of cereals and other food crops as well. Some of these are grown for us to eat while others provide food for cattle and other animals. Many crops are grown for the oil in their seeds. Examples include sunflowers, linseed, lupins and rape. The latter turns many fields brilliant yellow in the spring.

Below: This agricultural scene has been created entirely by people and their animals. Crops are grown in most of the fields, but cattle graze on the rougher grassland in the foreground.

COMMON CROPS

Maize

Oilseed Rape

Sugar Beet

Wheat

Barley

Oats

Index

Editor: Vanessa Clarke
Designer: Ben White
Illustrators: Wendy Brammall, Martin Camm, Denys Ovenden, Alan MaLe, Jeane Colville, Gordon Riley, Bernard Robinson, Ann Winterbotham and David Wright.
Cover Design: Pinpoint Design Company

Photographs: page 14 NHPA/Stephen Dalton; 15 Nature Photographers *top*; 17 NHPA/R.J. Erwin; 21 NHPA/Lacz Lemoine; 23 Pat Morris; 24 Nature Photographers *bottom*; 25 Nature Photographers *top and bottom;* 31 ZEFA; all other photographs: Michael Chinery.

First published in 1985 by Kingfisher Books Limited, Elsley Court, 20–22 Great Titchfield Street, London W1P 7AD
A Grisewood & Dempsey Company

Text Copyright © Michael Chinery 1985
Illustrations Copyright © Kingfisher Books Ltd 1985

BRITISH LIBRARY CATALOGUING IN PUBLICATION DATA
Chinery, Michael
    Fields and Hedgerows, – (Exploring the countryside)
    1. Natural history – Great Britain – Juvenile literature   2. Meadow fauna – Great Britain – Juvenile literature   3. Hedgerow ecology – Great Britain – Juvenile literature
    I. Title   II. Series
    574.941   QH137
ISBN: 0 86272 148 2

Phototypeset by Southern Posities and Negatives (SPAN), Lingfield, Surrey
Printed in Italy by Vallardi Industrie Grafiche, Milan